GOD'S WONDERFUL WORLD OF NUMBERS
TWO ENORMOUS ELEPHANTS

Glenda Palmer and Steve Henry

Chariot Books™
David C. Cook Publishing Co.

Dear Parents,

Remember how delighted your children were when they first learned to say their numbers from one to ten?

Now you can help them take the next step! As you read *Two Enormous Elephants* together, you can help your kids learn to count, not just have the numbers memorized. Before you know it, they'll look at the fish in the tank and tell you that there are eight—or three cookies in the cookie jar, or six marbles in the bag.

So read *Two Enormous Elephants* time and time again, and help you children discover God's wonderful world of numbers.

Chariot Books™ is an imprint of David C. Cook Publishing Co.
David C. Cook Publishing Co., Elgin, Illinois 60120
David C. Cook Publishing Co., Weston, Ontario
Nova Distribution Ltd., Newton Abbot, England

TWO ENORMOUS ELEPHANTS: GOD'S WONDERFUL WORLD OF NUMBERS
© 1993 by Glenda Palmer for text and Steve Henry for illustrations

Designed by Elizabeth Thompson
First Printing, 1993
Printed in Singapore.
97 96 95 94 93 5 4 3 2 1

Palmer, Glenda.
Two enormous elephants : God's wonderful world of numbers / by Glenda Palmer.
          p.   cm.
Summary: A child praises God for creating a variety of creatures, from one human being to ten ladybugs.
ISBN 0-7814-0709-5
1. Counting—Juvenile Literature. [1. Counting. 2. Animals. 3. Christian life.]
I. Title II. Title: 2 enormous elephants.
QA1113.P346 1993
513.2'11—dc20
[E]   92-34714
                                                                    CIP
                                                                    AC

I know all about numbers!

I can count and point from **1 to 10**.

1 2 3 4 5
6 7 8 9 10

But millions of good things come from Him!

One is for me.

One is for you, too. In this big, wide, wonderful world, God liked you so much He made only one person exactly like you. You!

Thank You, God, for making us.

Two is for these enormous elephants living in the zoo.

Thank You for elephants, God. Thank You for giving me **two** eyes to see how big they are and **two** ears to hear how loud they sound and **two** arms to wave to them and **two** legs to walk around the zoo.

Three fuzzy brown bears live in the forest under **three** trees. **Three** funny stuffed bears live in my room.

God, I thank You for bears. Some are a little bit scary, and some make me laugh. Do they make You laugh too?

Four cows moo-moo-moo-moo in the barnyard of this farm. Each cow is wearing a cowbell and has a baby calf standing beside her. **Four** cows. **Four** cowbells. **Four** calves.

Thank You, God, for cows that moo and give me milk. Cold and yummy milk. Especially with my **four** animal crackers.

Five frisky puppies yip-yip-yip-yip-yip and tumble in the grass. See the **five** red rubber bones they chew on?

I like to play with puppies, God. I think You do too.

I can point and count
from **1** to **5**!

1

2

3

4

5

Six ducks float in a row. Quack-quack-quack-quack-quack-quack.

Thank You, God, for quacking ducks. It's fun to watch them dive in the cold water and gobble up the **six** pieces of bread I feed them.

Seven squirrels scamper on **seven** branches of an oak tree in the park. Count the nuts they found.

Thank You, God. I like to watch squirrels playing in their tree house.

Eight shimmering goldfish swim. **Eight** sandy seashells sparkle in the bottom of the tank. See the **eight** air bubbles bubble-bubble?

Thank You, God, for goldfish. I like to watch them swim.

Nine bees buzzzzz around the flowers, gathering nectar to make **nine** jars of licky, sticky sweet honey.

Thank You for honeybees, too, dear God, even if one did sting me once. Thank You for teaching them to make honey for me to put on my toast.

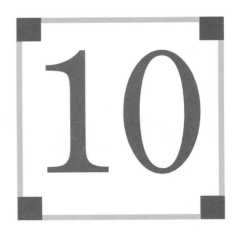

Ten daisies with **ten** yellow middles bloom
in the sunshine. Just enough for a bouquet!
Ten ladybugs fly away when I pick the daisies.

I can point and count
from 1 to 10,

2

3

4

5

6

7

8

9

10

but millions,

and millions and millions of good things come from Him. Thank You, God. You're the greatest!